Simple Techniques
for Complex
Projects

Deep Relief
Wood Carving

Kevin Walker

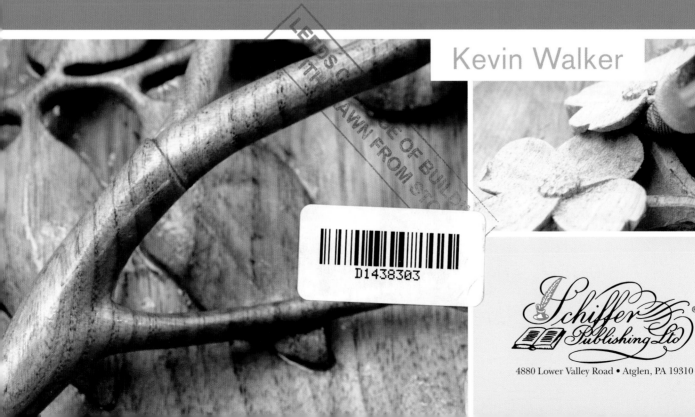

Schiffer Publishing Ltd

4880 Lower Valley Road • Atglen, PA 19310

Other Schiffer Books on Related Subjects

**Relief Carving
with Nora Hall**
Nora Hall
978-0-7643-3938-7

**Practical
Woodcarving:
Design and Application**
James E. Seitz
978-0-7643-1690-6

**Relief Carving
with Bob Lundy:
Scenery in Wood**
Bob Lundy
978-0-88740-439-9

Published by Schiffer Publishing, Ltd.
4880 Lower Valley Road
Atglen, PA 19310
Phone: (610) 593-1777; Fax: (610) 593-2002
E-mail: Info@schifferbooks.com

For our complete selection of fine books on this and related
subjects, please visit our website at www.schifferbooks.com.
You may also write for a free catalog.

This book may be purchased from the publisher.
Please try your bookstore first.

We are always looking for people to write books on new
and related subjects. If you have an idea for a book,
please contact us at proposals@schifferbooks.com.

Schiffer Publishing's titles are available at special discounts
for bulk purchases for sales promotions or premiums. Special
editions, including personalized covers, corporate imprints,
and excerpts can be created in large quantities for special needs.
For more information, contact the publisher.

CONTENTS

Preface

Relief carving always begins with a flat slab of wood. The background remains solid as you carve, hence the term relief. This makes the piece more difficult, but in the end, more beautiful.

My wife and I began going to Branson, Missouri, in the early 1980s, when vendors displayed relief wood carvings up and down Highway 76 and in Silver Dollar City. I was amazed by the undercutting, the wood's beauty, and the way the design lifted off a flat background, giving it a three-dimensional look. I bought my first set of tools at Silver Dollar City in 1982 and have been carving ever since.

My first piece was a simple pattern inspired by the poem "The Legend of the Dogwood." I carved the pattern several times, each time with more detail and depth. After experimenting with various types of wood, I developed a preference for butternut (white walnut). Through the years, my relief designs kept getting deeper and more complex. For me, the most intriguing aspects of deep relief work are layering and undercutting.

Deep relief carving requires a knowledge of both gouges and pressure. You will develop an understanding of wood grain direction and how much pressure to apply. The key is to take your time, because the pieces grow more fragile as you work. Somehow, the difficulty offers the potential to take it to the next level. *The bigger the challenge, the more potential there is for something truly special.*

In my seminars, I often start by asking students, "Would you rather make fifty carvings of mediocre quality or one Best of Show?" The response is usually the same—they would rather carve one Best of Show. This book offers a pattern and detailed instructions for making an intricate, three-dimensional sculpture in a 2" thick flat piece of butternut. The biggest challenge will be not to hurry, but to allow yourself time to hone your skills and reflect on what Best of Show quality means. You can make this project easier or more challenging by modifying the cutting depth as you plan your strategy.

The book also includes a simpler 9×12" relief dogwood pattern that you can use while following the main lesson. I encourage beginners to practice with a small stem before attempting to carve the main subject of this book. With that 9×12" piece, you can go a little less deep and use less undercutting to develop your skills.

I believe wood sculpture should reflect the artist's passion and point of view, and that it should not be reproduced for sale. While I have nothing against commercial artwork, I prefer a purist approach because that's what stirs my soul—experiencing the wood grain's look and texture and the sharpness of the gouges and hand tools. I enjoy the precision with which you can move a gouge through a piece of wood. Wood lends itself to becoming relatively fragile, while still remaining intact and strong. It always tells you how to treat it, but you have to do a lot of study and a little carving. I like finely detailed sculpture and the fact that the finer you sand a piece of wood, the more power you give the grains. They are richer, cleaner, and crisper, and the carving takes a finish better. These qualities make wood the ideal medium. It's warm, and it draws you away from the daily hustle and bustle. Allow it to speak to you.

Acknowledgments

Thanks to my daughter, Shannan Walker, for her help with photography and for turning my chicken scratch into text. I am also grateful to Heritage Portraits for their photography assistance, and to Jeannie Starr for her careful proofreading eye.

Chapter 1

DRAWING THE DESIGN

Figures 1.1-1.2: Before carving a dogwood blossom, I went outside and plucked several variations of the bracts to study. You have to be quick about doing this in springtime because dogwood blooms fade quickly. It seems like a simple little flower, but when you attempt to duplicate anything Mother Nature has made there will be problems, especially when you are converting a flower to a piece of wood. One of the challenges is keeping it symmetrical; it's not as easy as it appears.

Study how the bloom looks in nature, and then cut out your own pattern variation from a simple freehand drawing. If you are uncomfortable drawing freehand, use a scale to guide the proportions.

When you do repetitive carving, it's a good idea to make a pattern or jig using a band saw and a thin piece of wood. One dogwood bloom is pretty much the same size and shape as another, and the cutout helps to keep everything symmetrical (Figure 1.2).

On my pattern, you will notice that parts of the dogwood bloom are not perfectly true to form. I strive for expression in my designs, not duplication. I don't believe anyone can duplicate nature, and I don't see the point of it, anyway. When somebody recognizes it as a dogwood, you will have served the subject well.

In the past, when I carved the stamens as they appeared in nature, I wasn't satisfied with the outcome. I also modified the design because their little bitty

Figure 1.1

Original Design by Kevin Walker

Dogwood stem pattern

spires are difficult to carve. I use a small diamond bit to concave each stamen and carve folds in some of the dogwood petals to add character and realism. These elements give the work my signature and personality.

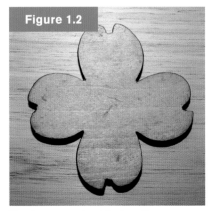

Figure 1.2

Bandsaw wooden blank pattern

Constructing the Pattern

Figure 1.3

Example of artist corrections pattern

Figure 1.3: Curves are beautiful. If a dogwood stem doesn't have curves, add them. The stems should have a lot of curves and the blooms should turn away from each other. The section joints in the dogwood stem are beautiful, too, and help to identify dogwood varieties. Articulating them gives you an opportunity to add a little stain to the area. The leaf patterns are meant to be realistic, though they are manipulated slightly. It's important to offset the leaves; otherwise they look too consistent and phony. The goal is a design that flows and has depth, motion, and balance. You want surprise and distortion. The clusters may appear wind-blown.

Start by drawing a curved line that will represent the stem. Then trace your dogwood flower jig, turning it and tracing more blooms around it. Keep the blooms ½" or so from the edges and consider the depth of your piece as you're laying out your design.

Chapter 2

TOOL TIPS

When I carved my first few pieces, I did not have the tool collection I have now. The point is, you can carve this piece without many of the tools described in the next chapters.

HOWEVER, THE FOLLOWING TOOLS FROM WOODCRAFT ARE ESSENTIAL FOR BEGINNERS

1. Ramelson palm-handled carving set (order #09I20)

2. 6 mm back-bend gouge (order #05F70)

3. 12 mm #3 and 14 mm #7 sweep spoon gouge (order #05K03 and 05K11)

4. 20 mm bent gouge (order #05508)

5. 14 mm #3 sweet fishtail gouge (order #05M06)

6. Rick Butz carving knife (A) 18522

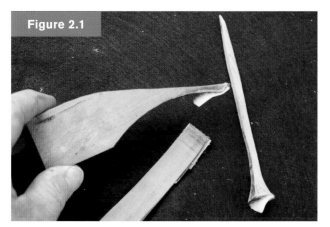
Figure 2.1

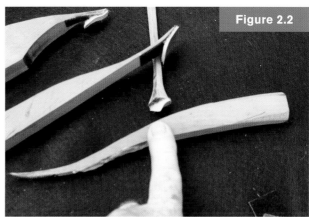
Figure 2.2

Sanding tools

Figures 2.1-2.2: I have also developed a set of three tools for sanding the background and under stems and leaves.

I cut the tools from a piece of wood in the shape of a bent gouge, then attach sandpaper with Velcro. You can build these yourself or order them from me at 479-474-0813 or 479-459-0813.

Sandpaper is simply another tool that takes skill to use, like a gouge or power tool. Learn to shape your sandpaper to accommodate the item you are sanding.

Figure 2.3

Proper sandpaper technique

Figures 2.3-2.5: Sanding underneath fragile parts of your carving, such as a stem part, is easy once you develop the soft touch. Cut a ¼"-wide strip of 220 grit and use gently.

Carving hard-to-reach areas, such as between the stems and leaf clusters, can be challenging. Use small diamond bits for clean-out. Then maneuver a small, straight gouge straight in, scraping out the finished background. The cut should be sharp and straight, or at a slight bevel.

This carving is done with a single piece of wood.

However, you may want to use up smaller pieces of stock and will have to laminate, or glue, edge to edge. The quality will not suffer if lamination is done correctly. Be sure to match up the grains as best you can. The grain patterns are cupped; place one piece cupped up and the next piece cupped down to prevent warping, but do not sacrifice color and clarity. Use a hand plane on stock pieces 2" or thicker. Clamp your pieces and find the grain direction. After planing, put the two pieces together and shine a flashlight on the joint to detect if light is passing through. Make corrections as needed for a flush fit before gluing.

Figure 2.4

Sanding underneath the stem

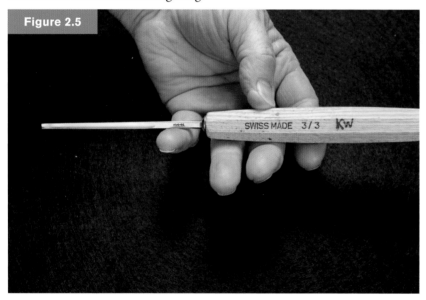

Figure 2.5

3/3 straight gouge

Chapter 3

ROUTER TEMPLATE

Transferring the Pattern onto a Wood Blank

Place good-quality carbon paper face down on the wood slab, keeping it at least ⅛" from the edge so you can tape it securely on all four sides. The 11¾×16" pattern provided is slightly smaller than the wood blank to accommodate taping. It must be patterned onto the wood perfectly, so take your time. Use a different color ink than the pattern so you can see where you traced. Firmly trace one field until it is fully patterned off. When finished, lift up the pattern carefully from the bottom, checking to see whether you've missed a line here or there. If you haven't removed the top, you can return it to the same position and make the corrections.

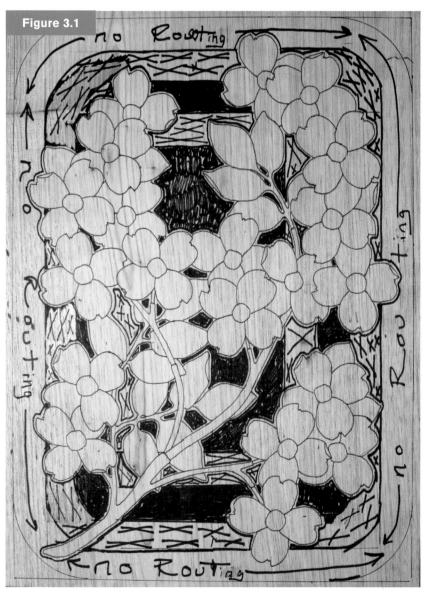

Figure 3.1

Figures 3.1-3.2: After removing the pattern and carbon paper, retrace the lines with a fine felt-tip pen. I cannot overemphasize that your lines must be clearly defined, because the router will create a lot of dust. I recommend the super-fine Sharpie˙ pictured here because it doesn't bleed.

Blank after pattern transfer

Figure 3.2

Sharpie pen

Figure 3.3

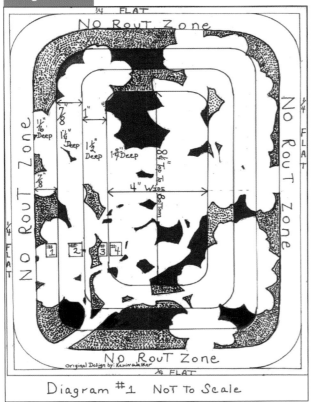

Diagram #1   NoT To Scale

Layout for router work

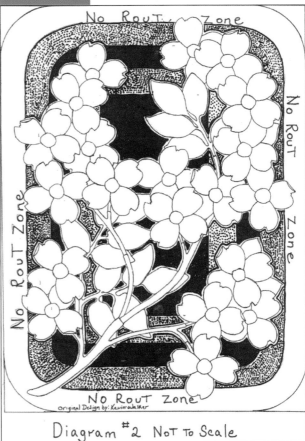

Diagram #2   NoT To Scale

Colored and dotted router guide

Figures 3.3-3.4: In figure 3.3, the stem is whited out to show the guide marks for routing the 11¾×16" blank. Make a mark at the center, then mark off 2" on each side, or 4" across. Now mark the vertical dimension. Starting at the center of your slab, measure 4⅛" in each direction, resulting in an area measuring 8 ¼ " from top to bottom. This 4×8¼" area will be routed to the deepest level at 1¾" (section #4). Moving horizontally and vertically, section #3 is 1" wide and 1½-" deep; section #2 is ⅞ " wide and 1¼" deep, and section #1 is ⅞" wide and ¹¹⁄₁₆" deep. The outer no-rout section tapers to zero and must be beveled with a hand gouge. The taper stops ¼" from the edge to accommodate a handmade or store-bought frame.

Now clearly mark each section to distinguish them while routing. Use a black marker to color in the central 4 ×8¼" section. Place dots in the adjacent section, followed by solid black and dots for the remaining two sections.

This template allows flexibility in undercutting the dogwood stem. It has a flat bottom, so you can choose the depth of any given area and create a tapered look. The idea is to make the background look soft, natural, and smooth, as if you had laid a dogwood stem on a piece of wood.

When routing, stop ⅛" short of any line drawing. It is better to leave too much wood at this point than risk touching your subject with a router bit.

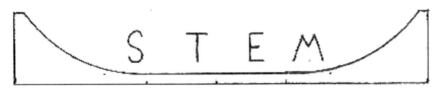

Stem ½-scale

Chapter 4

ROUTING OUT THE PERIMETER

Figure 4.1

Porter cable router

Figure 4.2

Bosch drill bit

Choosing Your Router

Figure 4.1: I use a fixed-base Porter Cable 1001 with a 5¾" type 8 router base. This is a heavy-duty router that performs well without vibrations and skips. If you use a router with a smaller base, be careful not to let it fall into the holes or tilt the base while you are routing. Depths are achieved by twisting the base, and a locking bracket locks it in.

Router Bits

Figure 4.2: I use a Bosch ¼×1" bit—a solid carbide, two-flute, down-cut spiral. It is a fast cutter and won't grab the wood when you go straight in. As a substitute, you may use a ¼" carbide straight bit. (In some areas, you will go straight down like a drill and not rout out beyond ¼". If you are going straight in on a small area and don't need to cut out anything beyond that, use a drill.) Measure the desired depth and tape around the drill bit to create a stopping point.

Routing Out the Blank

Figure 4.3: Beginning with the center level (#4, color-coded black as shown in figure 3.4), set the router to ¼" to shave off the first layer. At this point you might say, "I know my router can go to ½" or ¾". Be patient, because you are going to need that mindset throughout this project. Routing down to 1¾" in ¼" increments tears up less wood and gives you better control. If you hit your pattern, you will have to glue up another blank and start over. That is gospel. An easy way to accomplish this is to mark ¼" increments on the edge of your 2" wood base.

Area #3, coded with dots, is 1½" deep. Dust will fly, so keep an air hose handy or turn your blank upside down occasionally to remove the dust. To help you hit all your holes at the right depth, use a different color marker to number them in each section. Area #3 has 12 holes and several are small, so I recommend using a drill bit taped at 1½".

Use the same process in section #2, color-coded black, to rout 1¼" deep, and in section #1 to rout ¹¹⁄₁₆" deep. In this large area a ¼" straight bit and router will do the job and be easy to control.

After routing in the background, rough-in the leaf clusters, beginning at a ¼" depth. The leaf clusters sit beneath everything else, so rout them deeply to achieve a layered look. Rout 1¼" deep on the bottom two clusters and 1" deep on the top cluster.

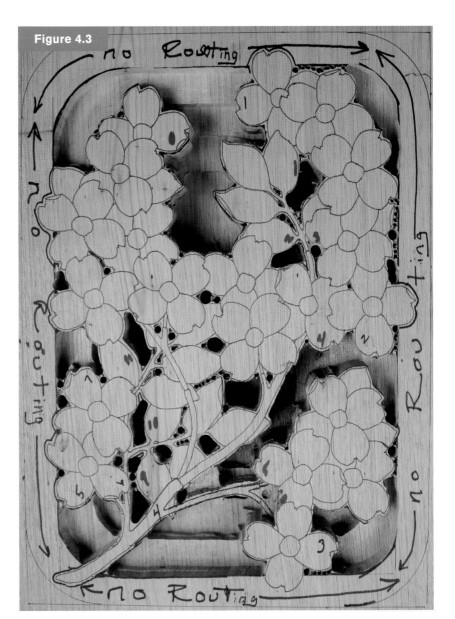

Figure 4.3

Routed blank up to this point

Chapter 5

CARVING OUT THE BACKGROUND

THE TOOLS USED IN THIS CHAPTER ARE AVAILABLE FROM WOODCRAFT.

1. 20mm fishtail #5 sweep F/20 (order #05 m13). Use: Quick rough-out.

2. 12mm fishtail #3 sweep 3 F/12 (order #05 m5). Use: Smoothing rough-out after the background is ready for sanding.

3. 6mm fishtail #3 sweep 3 F/16 (order #05 m26). Use: Same as previous tool, but for tighter spaces.

4. 12mm bent gouge #5 sweep 5L/12 (order #05NO). Use: To rough out corners with a con-cave shape top-to-bottom and side-to-side.

5. 16mm straight gouge #2 Sweep (order #05B09). Use: Outline flowers and stop cuts. Remem-ber to go straight down and stop the depth short of your final background. Use with mallet. **TIP**: Use sweep to your advan-tage by turning it around to fit the shape of your petals.

6. 8mm straight gouge #5 sweep (order #05D03). Use: For tight spaces and quick digging. **TIP**: Use your mallet for better con-trol, even with small tools.

7. 5mm straight gouge #5 sweep 3/5 (order #05605). Use: Multi-purpose; great for touch-ups.

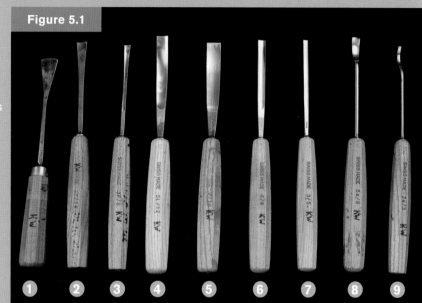

Figure 5.1

Figure 5.2

Figures 5.1-5.2: Tools used to cut in background

8. 8mm spoon gouge #5 sweep 5 A/8 (order #05K02). Use: Dig out background between flowers 15 and 17. Keeps your hand or tool from getting in the way when removing wood in high-relief areas.

9. 3mm spoon gouge #3 sweep 3 A/3 (order #03W55). Use: Tight spots between flower and stem. Similar to tool 8 but can reach even tighter areas.

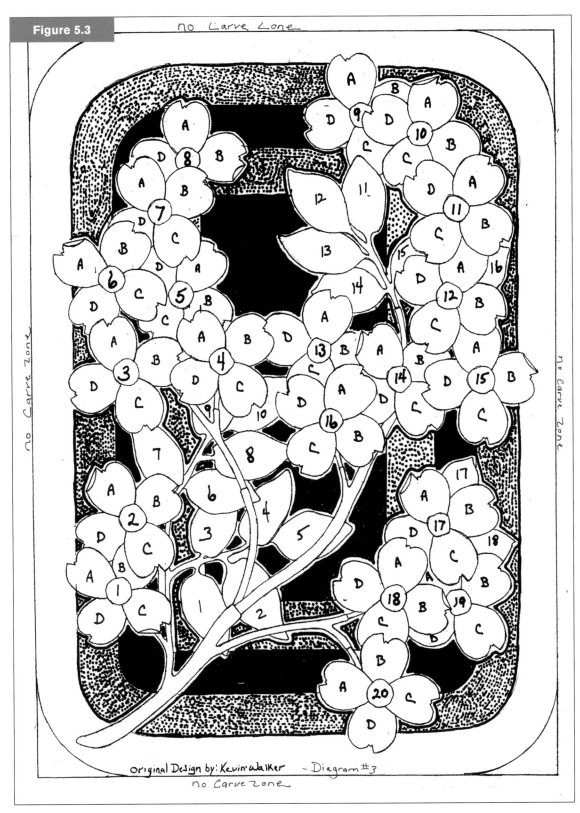

Figure 5.3

Numbered and lettered design

Cutting Out the Background

Figure 5.3: Read this entire chapter before beginning the background, and refer to figure 5-3 throughout. Staying ¼" from the edges, start at the top center. There is 1¼" between the top two dogwood blooms with which to start a bowl-shaped slope to the deepest part of the background. Use the router benches to gouge your depth (figure 5.4). Figure 5.5 shows the benchmark after it is carved.

Figure 5.4

Gauging the depth with router benches

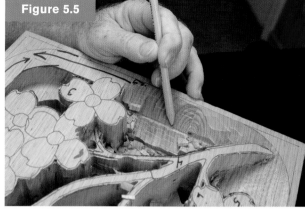

Figure 5.5

Depth guide

Figure 5.6

Beveled Slope

Beveled slope

Figure 5.7

Bowl Shape (Concave)

Bowl shape

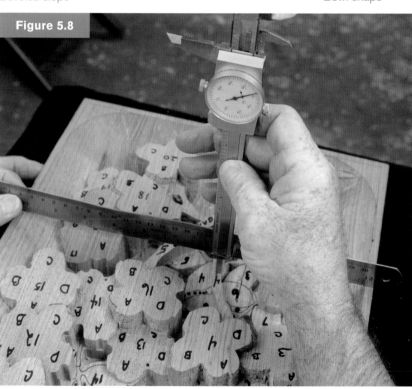

Figure 5.8

Measuring the depth

Figures 5.4-5.8: Once the bench edge is carved out, you will be at a bevel slope (figure 5.6). In the next steps, your fingers will tell you more than your eyes. Carve a little, then look at it and feel it until it takes on a bowl shape (figure 5.7). To gauge whether your cuts are consistent from one section to another, place one finger in one area and another in the other area; with a little practice, your brain will feel any differences. You can also use a measuring device to check for appropriate depth as you go around (figure 5.8).

Be careful not to go too deep with your stop cuts, and do not cut under any part of the drawing at this stage. Use a mallet with your gouge to cut around the blooms, staying outside the traced lines.

Roughing In the Blooms

Figure 5.9: Roughing in the blooms will lower them, giving you more access to carving the background. I slant each bloom a different way to make them look realistic. As you cut in the flowers, the stops stay flat.

> **TIP:** The more depth from bloom to bloom, the more movement you will create. Flowers tucked under each other work the imagination.

Figure 5.9

Stop cuts

Dogwood Flowers

Figures 5.10-5.11: Starting on the left side with **flower 2**, cut it in, turning down to about ⅛" from the background.

Figure 5.10

Cutting in flowers 1 and 2

Flower 1 turns down to the left to meet the background. The right side stays to the top at petal C.

Figure 5.11

Cutting in blooms 17, 18, 19, and 20

Figure 5.12

Finished background

Flower 20. Turn petal D down toward the background and keep petals A and B toward the top.

Flower 18 will be your highest in this cluster. Stay to the top of petal B; petal C tucks under **flower 20**. Petal D turns down only about

¼" from the top to allow room to tuck the stem under this flower cluster.

Flower 19. Turn petals C & B to about ⅛" from the background. This bloom tucks under **flowers 18** and **17**.

Flower 17. Turn this flower down toward the top of the carving, about ½" from the top of **flower 18** petal A. Petals D and C tuck under **flower 18** petal A at about ³⁄₁₆" deep.

Chapter 6

STYLIZING YOUR DESIGN & ROUGHING IN THE STEM

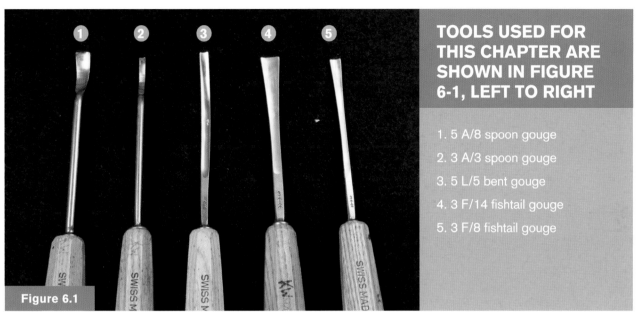

TOOLS USED FOR THIS CHAPTER ARE SHOWN IN FIGURE 6-1, LEFT TO RIGHT

1. 5 A/8 spoon gouge
2. 3 A/3 spoon gouge
3. 5 L/5 bent gouge
4. 3 F/14 fishtail gouge
5. 3 F/8 fishtail gouge

Figure 6.1

Tools used for stylizing your design

To keep it stable, the stem must be solidly attached to the background in several places. Consider the degree of difficulty you are willing to tackle. The higher you stay off the background, the more undercutting work you will have. The pattern shows that **flower 1** must be the deepest in its area.

Starting with **flower 7**, cut petal A as low as possible to the background. Stop-cut with the mallet and 3 F/8 gouge between **flowers 7** and **8** to separate them.

Figure 6.2

Process for cutting in flower blank 8

Figure 6.2: Go straight down for your stop cuts, and cut the flower blank flat on top. This will make it easier to draw in the details later. On **flower 7**, cut petal C ⁹⁄₁₆" deeper than the top of petal B. Petal C is not visible because it is underneath petal B. Shape in **flower 8** until petal A is about ¹⁄₁₆" from the finished background.

Figure 6.3

Finished blank, flower 8

Figure 6.3 Flower 5: Stop-cut around **flowers 3, 4, 6,** and **7,** cutting **flower 5** the deepest in this part of the stem.

Relieving flower 5

Figures 6.4-6.5: The deeper you go with **flower 5**, the more room you will have to carve different levels of **flowers 3, 4, 6,** and **7**. I tilted **flower 5** to the right and cut the petals ⅜" from the background. On **flower 6**, petals C and D are ½ " higher than **flower 5**. Tilt petal A down until it touches the background. Caution: This steep tilt is tricky because of the grain changes and requires selecting the right tools. If you choose not to go down as deep, you can still follow all of the basic steps. The deeper you go down and the more tilt you add, the more realistic it will appear.

   Flower 7: Tilt this bloom back into **flower 6** and leave petal B as high as possible. Petal D is under **flower 6** and lies ⅜" from the top.

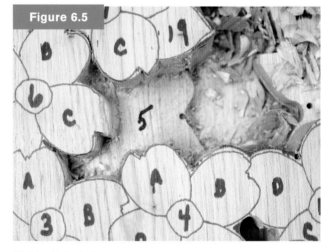

Finished blank, flower 5

Finished blank, flower 7

Figure 6.6: Flower 6: Tilt this bloom to the left. Cut down until petal A is almost even with the background. Leave the other side, petal C, as high as possible.

Finished blank, flower 6

Figures 6.7-6.8: Flower 3: I tilted petal C down to ½" from leaf 7 and petal A remains as high as possible. Feel free to make the carving your own; creating less tilt will be easier.

Finished blank, flower 3

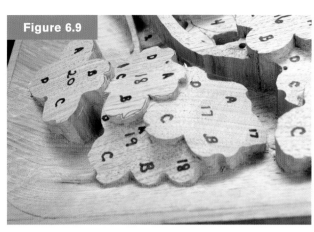

Flowers 17–20

Flowers 1 and 2

Flowers 3–8

Flowers 3–16

Measuring the depths

Figures 6.9-6.12: Flower 4: Tilt petals C and B down about ¼" and leave petal A at the top. Create a nice flat top where petals A and C meet.

Flower 9: Cut petal C down under leaf 11 and leave petal A at the top, tilting the bloom toward the bottom of the carving. This will differentiate it from flower 8 and add contrast.

Flower 10: Take petal B down deepest—to ¾" from the top. Keep petal D at the top and tilt the flower toward the right side of the carving.

Flower 12: Cut in petal A ⅜" below the top surface and keep petal C at the top. Carve this flower flat while keeping it tilted.

Flower 11: Cut in petal A ⅜" from the background. Keep petal

C to the top and tilt, leaving petal B at the top. This process will give this bloom a different turn, as opposed to flowers 10 and 12, creating a natural look.

Flower 13: Like flowers 5 and 13, this bloom needs to be cut in deep so that flowers 16, 14, and 15 will have depth flexibility. Stay about ⅝"below the surface of your carving when cutting in petals

C, D, and B. This depth will also add significantly to the overall dimension.

Flower 16: This bloom will stay at the top with petal A. Cut petal C in only about ¼" down and tilt the bloom in the direction of petal C, or to the lower leaf cluster.

Flower 14: This bloom will be cut in with no tilt and will be ⅜" from the top.

Flower 15: Cut petal B down to ⅛" from the background, keeping petal D at the top, and tilt entire flower toward the right.

Roughing In the Stem

Figures 6.13-6.14: We will stylize our stem to create drama and also make it seem to support the blooms correctly, while giving it plenty of support underneath.

I numbered all parts of the stem at their lowest levels. To measure the depth, set a straight edge across the top of the carving and a place a measuring tool on the stem where numbered (figure 6.13).

Figure 6.14

Numbered stem

You will notice that between numbers three and five is the word *grain* and two arrows. The arrow at the top of the stem points in the direction of the grain. The other arrow points down, indicating that the grain direction is going down and in the opposite direction. Knowing the direction of the wood grain is very important, especially for the stem. When possible, carve with the direction of the grain. Pushing your gouge against the grain puts a lot of pressure on the stem. The wood grain changes quickly; therefore the stem will break if you aren't careful.

Now for the stem depths:
- 1 is ¾" from the top
- 2 is 1¼" from the top
- 3 is ⅛" from the top
- 4 is ⅞" from the top
- 5 is ¾" from the top

Give the stems lots of bend as they are connecting to the back of the flower. Make sure each part of your stem has nice curves. If you are not careful, you may be inclined toward straight lines.

Chapter 7

DEFINING & SHAPING LEAF CLUSTERS

Figure 7.1: Use the depth diagram when carving out between the leaf clusters.

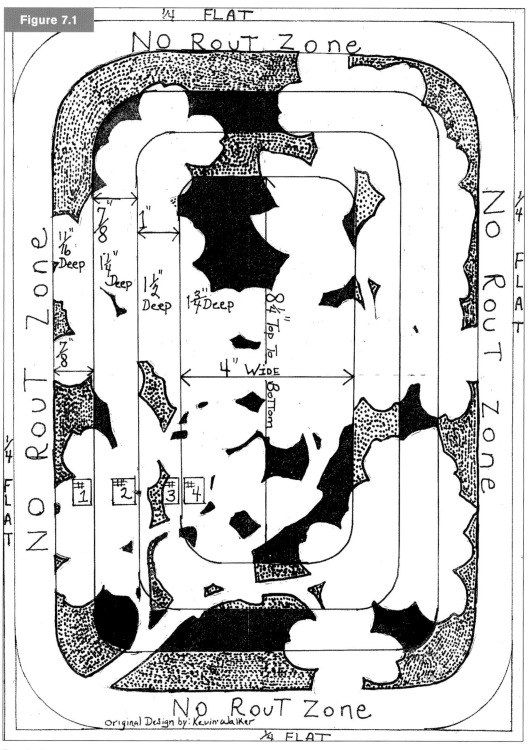

Figure 7.1

Depth diagram   **Not to Scale**

Measuring depth

Figure 7.2: First we will cut out between the leaves and stems, keeping the correct background depth. When the background curves up (bowl shape), use a straight edge and measuring device to keep in check.

I will be using various hand and power tools to dig out between the leaves.

5mm bent gouge 5 L/5

Figure 7.3: 5 mm bent gouge 5 L/5. This tool will be the largest in this area. Get all you can with this tool before moving to the next smaller tool.

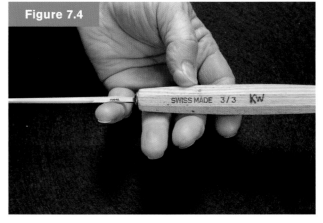

3/3 straight gouge

Figure 7.4: 3/3 straight gouge. This tool has a very small width. You will use it to outline your leaves in tight areas, but you can also go in straight down and scrape the bottom to get a smooth finish on the background when gouging is not possible.

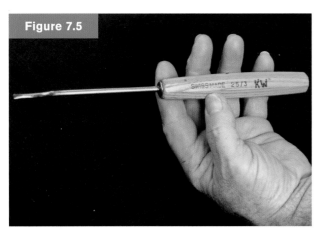

²⁵⁄₃ backbend

Figure 7.5: ²⁵⁄₃ backbend. This tool is great for undercutting and hard-to-reach areas.

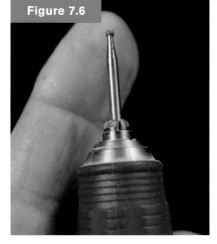

¹⁄₁₆" diamond ball

Figure 7.6: Small ¹⁄₁₆" diamond ball. Use this tool for finishing small background areas in even harder-to-reach areas.

Figure 7.7

Figure 7.8

Figure 7.9

Figure 7.7-7.9: ¼" burr. This tool will take large amounts of wood out in a hurry, so be careful. In the next image, I am relieving from **flowers 4** and **16** to expose the leaf underneath. Do not take more than you must, or your blooms may be too thin to carve. Leave at least ¼" for the thickness of **flowers 4** and **16**.

Figures 7.7-7.9: Relieving from flowers 4 and 16

Figure 7.10

Figure 7.11

Figures 7.10-7.11: Undercutting the stem

Figures 7.10-7.11: ⅛ " burr. Next, relieve **flowers 1** and **2** and some of the stem above **leaves 1, 2,** and **5** using a ¼" burr and a ⅛" burr. This will create better access to the leaf cluster.

When you have relieved your blooms and leaves out somewhat, look at your pattern, redraw the stem line, and shape the stem parts around **flowers 1** and **2**. Then clean out around the stem parts.

Do not try to make anything look finished at this point. If you do, the dimensions will change. I know this may try your patience, but it will pay off in the end.

¹⁄₁₆" **round carbide bit.** The stem below **flower 1** forks off and the left part is higher than the right stem section. Tilt this part in to the right while keeping the left side much higher. The right side of the stem goes under **flowers 1** and **2.** Draw in the stem again. Use a ¹⁄₁₆" round carbide bit to clean out between these two stem sections.

Figure 7.12

Redrawing the stem line

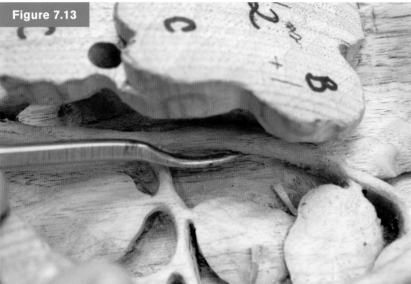

Figure 7.13

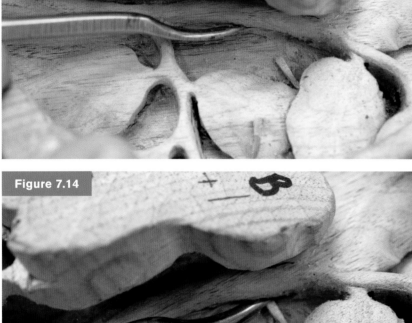

Figure 7.14

Figures 7.13-7.15: Clean-out around the stem parts

Figure 7.15

TIP: If your tool will not move through the wood without damaging another part, stop and rethink your tool choice or your entry. Remember to use the largest tool possible and the smallest tool necessary.

Figure 7.16

Figure 7.17

Figure 7.18

Figures 7.16-7.18: Shaping the leaves

Figure 7.19

Cleaning the background

Leaf Shaping

Figures 7.16-7.19: Begin carving your leaves in a convex shape, but give each leaf its own personality. Use small bent gouges and straight gouges to perform this task. Trim around the leaves as you shape them and clean up the background around your leaves.

As you get into tight areas, use the small carbide bit where the stem and leaves meet. Use 220-grit sandpaper to smooth rough areas. Cut it into small pieces and fold the paper to create a sharp edge for sanding. Don't sand too well at this point. You will redraw the leaf veins in and finish carving in the detail next.

Detailing Leaf Veins

Figures 7.20-7.23: Draw in the center of each leaf vein, and then take a small veiner palm tool and carve shallow scores on both sides of your drawing. Smooth out the veins by rounding them on both sides, then sand lightly with 220-grit sandpaper.

Roughed in leaf section

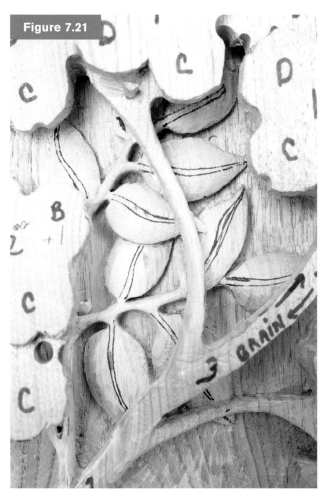

Drawing the leaf veins

Relieving the veins

Rounding off the leaf veins

Creating a Ripple in Your Leaf

Figure 7.24: Use a small palm gouge to dig out the leaf edges at random, leaving some leaves intact. Soften the gouge marks with a 2mm or 3mm straight gouge and sand lightly.

Undercutting the Bottom Leaf Cluster

Figures 7.25-7.29: When undercutting the bottom leaf cluster and stem section, it's important to understand how the underside should look. The underneath won't be finished, but I try to make it neat because that's what everyone loves to look at. A burry, trashy finish is not acceptable, so if you go too deep to create a neat look, you are going in too far. The goal is that when you peer in, you see the dogwood stem and a nicely hollowed out background.

Your leaf cluster is low to the background, so you will use a wedge undercutting technique for most of the leaves. Use a small carbide ball on the stem at the leaf base and finish with a small backbend tool, then sand lightly with 220-grit sandpaper.

Mark the side of the stem to keep its depth and width proportionate. The stems on a dogwood tree are round. Finish by sanding lightly with 220-grit sandpaper. Then take your bent gouges and complete the final background cleanup around the bottom leaf cluster.

Figure 7.24

Finished lower leaf cluster

Figure 7.25

Figure 7.26

Figures 7.25-7.26: Wedge out with backbend gouge

Figure 7.27

Figure 7.28

Figures 7.27-7.28: Finishing with power

Final background clean-up

Stem

Figures 7.30-7.31: Round the top of the main stem directly above the leaf cluster you just finished.

Figures 7.30-7.31: Rounding over the main stem

Figure 7.32

Figure 7.33

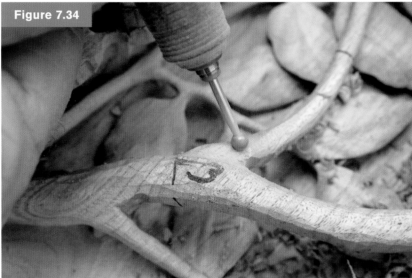

Figure 7.34

Figures 7.32-7.34: The stem forks off (#3) and also has a joint at this section. Drop the smaller joint down about ¹⁄₁₆" with a ⅛" diamond bit. After shaping this stem section, redraw the details according to the pattern.

Figures 7.32-7.34: Diamond bit demonstration

Figure 7.35

Figure 7.35: Stop-cut your lines using a detail knife. Cut back the stems above the main section to give the illusion that they slip into the main section.

Drawing the stem details

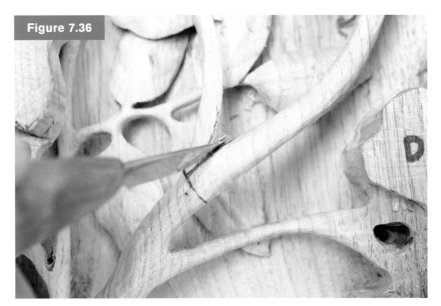

Figure 7.36

Stop-cutting with a knife

Figures 7.36-7.41: The stem sections off several more times. Follow the pattern and the previous steps. Carve the smaller stems slightly lower where they branch off. These stems are smaller in diameter. Do not carve the area where they go directly into dogwood blooms yet. You want to have plenty of meat left on the bones in case the pitch varies as you finish carving the blooms.

Figure 7.37

Cross-cuting with a knife

Figure 7.38

Creating the joint

Figure 7.39

Creating the joint

Figure 7.40

Tapering the joint

Figure 7.41

Finished stem joint

Figure 7.42

Finished stem

Upper Leaf Cluster

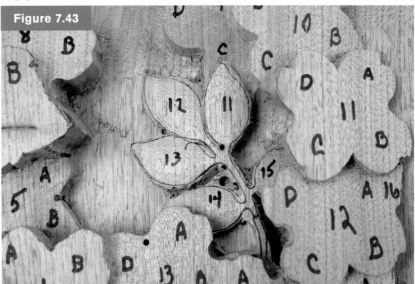

Figure 7.43: The upper leaf cluster will be raised more in the center, but will drop at the leaf tips. As we rough the cluster into a convex shape, make sure the leaf tips on numbers 12, 13, and 14 touch the background. Then use the template or redraw this leaf cluster in freehand.

Redrawn leaf cluster

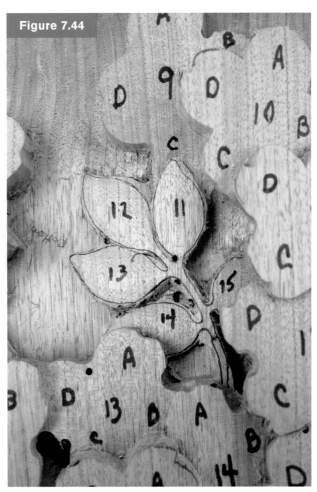

Finished upper leaf cluster

Figures 7.44-7.45: Repeat the same steps as with the lower cluster. Remember to cut between leaf 15 and flowers 11 and 12 with a ¼" burr so that you can carve all the leaves in the cluster. Give yourself plenty of room to get to this leaf. Remember, it will be mostly covered by blooms, so you don't have to carve it perfectly.

Chapter 8

CARVING THE DOGWOOD FLOWERS

After carving flowers 17–20 in step-by-step detail, you will know how to carve the remaining flowers.

Figures 8.1-8.2: Figure 8-1 shows a dotted line through the middle of the flower. This section cut is illustrated in figure 8-2. Viewed straight on, the flower petals look thinner than they really are. Make sure your petals are well supported and not too thin, so they don't break. The key to making the dogwood look dainty is to come out very thin at the petal tips. The top and the bottom must have a consistent shape, but thickness doesn't matter because both sides are not visible at the same time. Relief carving is not three-dimensional—there is no real subject matter on the underside. However, in high relief the undercutting and support work needs to be attractive. In fact, the undercutting work can and should have an appeal all its own.

In figure 8-2, area #2 shows the flower support. The stem should appear to be coming up beneath the flower center. The support

Dogwood Dissected

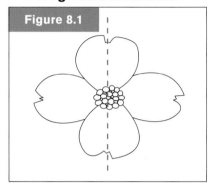

Dogwood Inside View

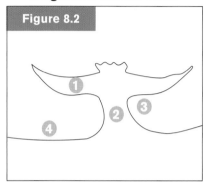

Figures 8.1-8.2: The dogwood dissected

does not have to be as thin as most of the stems, but, as I will show you, the support for the highest flowers will be as thin as the stem and add drama. Additional support will come from being connected at points to other flowers.

In area #3, there is enough room to finish most of your undercutting work with a ⅛" shank—approximately ¼" round Tungsten carbide burr. As I will demonstrate later in this chapter, this burr will create a nice concave shape and will give you most of

the smoothness required, since this area is mostly hidden and dark, especially when it is stained and finished. For a smoother look, use a large diamond bit after shaping with your burr bit.

Area #4 is the background. We will rough in this area with a power tool and finish with a bent gouge (#3 sweep) and sand. Cut with the grain when possible. You will be taking out very thin slices, which pulls the grain, causing pits that will force you to go deeper and deeper to get a smooth finish.

Wedge-Out Technique

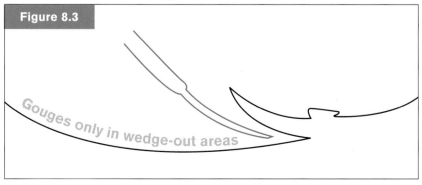

Gouges only in wedge-out areas

Figure 8.3: Figure 8-3 shows the wedging-out technique. The term wedging out means that the space under the flower meets the background at 0°. Power bits are not used when wedging out.

Stencil the Pattern

Using the stencil

Figure 8.4: Cut out a flower stencil from card stock using the pattern provided. You will be able to use this stencil throughout your carving, bending back the petals to accommodate any situation, as I will demonstrate later in this chapter.

Trim outline stencil

Figure 8.5: Always start with the highest flower in the cluster, because the undercutting work will expose other flowers. Starting with **flower 20**, use a 2 or 3 sweep (small gouges) to carve straight down along the stencil line. Go down roughly ¼". We will undercut later and taper to a point at the flower tip.

Trim outline stencil

Finished trim-out blank

Figures 8.6-8.7: Next, stop-cut about ¹⁄₁₆" deep between the petals and around the stamen. Your stop cuts should go down just far enough to start carving. You can go deeper as you relieve out the wood.

Carving Petal A

Figure 8.8
Stop-cutting the bloom

Figure 8.9
Stop-cutting the bloom

Figures 8.8-8.9: Use a small spoon gouge (palm tool) that fits nicely into the petal and creates a nice spoon shape.

Figure 8.10
Hump drawn in

Figure 8.10: Petals A and C, the under-petals, are roughed in first. Carve them before you carve the top petals to avoid breaking the top petals.

Draw in your lines, leaving a hump in the center of the petal. Carve the petals out in a spoon shape. Stay high at the tips and go lower where the petal meets the stamen, about ⅛" below the top of the stamen. Leave the hump at the center from the tip of the petal tapering down to the stamen; round over this hump.

Figure 8.11
Spoon gouge

Figure 8.11: While forming the spoon-like shape on the petal, carve in a circular motion and remember that this petal goes under the two top petals. Carve down about ⅛" below the top of the stamen.

Figures 8.12-8.17: Draw in lines to provide a guideline for a veiner tool.

Figure 8.12

Figure 8.13

Figure 8.14

Figure 8.15

Figures 8.12-8.15: Roughing in petal A

Figure 8.16

Figure 8.17

Finished rough-in petal A

Finished rough-in petals A & C

Carving Over Petals

Carve petals B and D basically the same as petals A and C, except they must appear to lie on top of the lower petals. Their edges should be a little higher than the lower petals.

Finished rough-in petals B and D

Round stamen

Figures 8.18-8.19: Round the stamen, but do not add detail yet.

Creating Ruffles in the Petals

Figures 8.20-8.22: A veiner tool is a U-gouge that is very narrow and very deep. Use it to carve out the petal's traced lines roughly ¹⁄₁₆" deep or less.

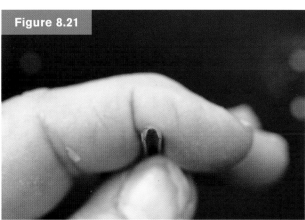

Figures 8.20-8.22: Veiner tool

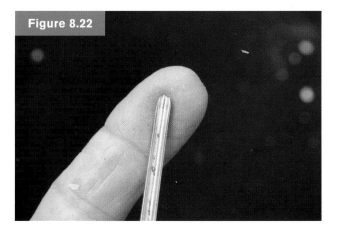

Figures 8.23-8.26: Rough in ruffles

Finished rough-in of ruffles with veiner tool

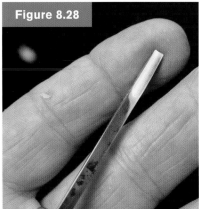

Palm tool (2mm)

Figures 8.28-8.29: Using the 2mm palm tool, feather the two outside ruffle grooves to the edges of each petal.

Rounding Over Ruffles

Figure 8.30-8.41: Roll a 2mm gouge over the sharp edges to create a softer, rounder ruffle like those you would find on a real dogwood blossom.

Figure 8.30

Figure 8.31

Figures 8.30-8.35: Carving outer edge (ruffle)

Figure 8.32

Figure 8.33

Figure 8.34

Figure 8.35

Figures 8.36-8.40: Rounding over the ruffles

Finished rough-in of ruffles

Sanding the Petals

Figures 8.42-8.50: I use 1½" strips of 220-grit Gator waterproof silicone carbide sandpaper to finish my dogwoods. This paper folds without splitting, allowing me to bend it into the folds and ruffles. Fold the sandpaper until it is about 1½" wide for easy control. Sand back and forth and side to side until the ruffle edges are soft, being careful not to sand a rut into the petal.

Cutting the sandpaper

Folding the sandpaper

Figures 8.46-8.49: Sanding the petals

Figure 8.48

Figure 8.49

Figure 8.50

Finished petals

Figures 8.51-8.61: Draw ⅛" circles on the flower center, starting on the outside. Cut a series of slits around each circle with a knife. Pull your knife from the outside edge to the inside edge of the stamen area to avoid breaking a piece. Cut just deep enough to take out a sliver of wood to separate the circles.

Power out the stamen circles with a ³⁄₁₆" diamond bit, using a light touch and a tapping action. Go down just far enough to define the outer edges of each circle.

Figure 8.51

Circles on stamen

Figure 8.52

Figures 8.52-8.53: Separating the stamen

Figure 8.53

Figure 8.54

Figures 8.54-8.56: Wedging out stamen A-B-C

Figure 8.55

Figure 8.56

Figure 8.57

Wedged-out stamen

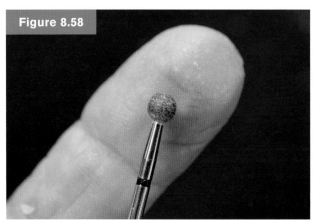

Figure 8.58

Diamond bit

Figure 8.59

Figure 8.60

Figures 8.59-8.61: Cupping the stamen

Figure 8.61

Figure 8.62

Figure 8.62: Petal B of flower 20 needs to be relieved underneath to access flower 18. Use any 2 or 3-sweep straight gouge and a narrow backbend gouge. See figure 8-1 at the chapter beginning for the petal thickness.

Finished stamen

Figures 8.63-8.72: Now we are ready to carve flower 18. It is slanted back into flower 20, presenting something of a challenge. Petal B of flower 20 is laying over petal C on flower 18. How you undercut petal B will dictate how petal C will meet flower 20. Use your stencil to trace out flower 18. Simply fold back petal C to avoid running into flower 20, then freehand the part you couldn't reach. Once you have most of the bloom traced, it will reveal how to draw the little bit that you couldn't trace on.

Carve petals A, B, and D like you did with flower 20. On petal C, you will need to compensate for petal B on flower 20 being in the way. With a gouge, go in sideways and carve from inside out. Use a diamond bit to finish carving what you couldn't reach with a gouge.

Figure 8.63

Figure 8.64

Figures 8.63-8.71: Wedging-out undercutting petal

Figure 8.65

Figure 8.66

Figure 8.67

Figure 8.68

Figure 8.69

Figure 8.70

Figure 8.71

Figure 8.72

Finished undercut petal B on flower 20

Figures 8.73-8.78: Mark all petals for your vein work and follow the finish instructions used for flower 20. I added an optional small fold in flower 18, which you can incorporate into any flower if you like.

Draw a line like my line in figure 8-77. Carve down a little deeper to create a fold, as shown in figure 8-78. Roll the fold over a little on both sides.

Figure 8.73

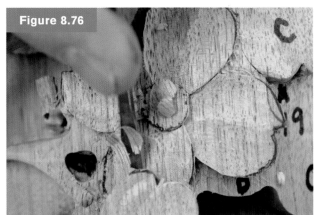

Figure 8.74

Figures 8.73-8.76: Side-to-side carving petal C

Figure 8.75

Figure 8.76

Figure 8.77

Leaf fold

Figure 8.78

Dropping down the petal

Figures 8.79-8.82: Pattern off **flower 17**, then relieve under petal A on flower 18. Carve **flower 17**. Petal D will not go under flower 18 very deep. Tuck the leaf under the bloom only about ⅛". Round the leaf over as you did with previous leaf clusters. Before stenciling **flower 19**, undercut all overlapping petals from **flowers 17** and **18**. This will give you more room to draw your blossom. You won't need to take out a lot, just wedge out without power and leave plenty of meat on the bones so that these petals will remain strong.

Figure 8.79

Figure 8.80

Figures 8.79-8.80: Creating a fold

Figure 8.81

Finishing undercutting of petal A on flower 18

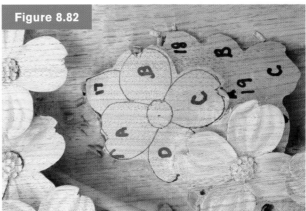

Figure 8.82

Stenciling flower 17

Figures 8.83-8.84: The undercutting work here will pattern after the cup shape on the petal's top side. Again, neatness and conformity matters more than the petal's thickness.

Figure 8.83

Figure 8.84

Figures 8.83-8.84: Wedging out flowers 17 and 18

Figure 8.85: Now we are ready to stencil **flower 19**. As you see here, you can bend, fold, twist, and even cut your stencil to accommodate any situation. Make more than one stencil, if necessary.

Stenciling flower 19

Finished stencil on flower 19

Figure 8.86: This flower's challenges will be a good example to refer back to as you work on the other flowers. It tilts and tucks under the two top flowers. One spot on petal A needs special attention. You will do some work on this petal with a ⅛" diamond bit to get to some of the areas under the flower. Outline around the stamen and all the petals, then separate the leaf. Go down about ⅛" from petal B and round the leaf over top. Use small gouges and be very careful not to touch the petal tips.

Rounding over the leaf

Powering out for separation

Figures 8.87-8.88: Shape petal B first, curving it up and into the stamen. This is an under-petal. Keep it cup-shaped and drop it down ⅛" below the stamen.

Figures 8.89-8.90: Petal D is harder to reach but can still be carved with the small spoon palm gouge.

Figure 8.89

Process flower 19, petal B

Figure 8.90

Finished petal B on flower 19

Figures 8.91-8.94: I also used a small backbend to wedge out. Pull the wood out with your gouge after making the wedge cut. Now for the over-petals: carve petal C first. There is nothing in your way here. Because of its pitch, you will learn a lot about cooperation with the wood grain.

Figure 8.91

Figure 8.92

Figures 8.91-8.94: Carving flower 19, petal D

Figure 8.93

Figure 8.94

Figures 8.95-8.96: Now for Petal A, the hardest in this cluster. Start against the grain with your small spoon gouge.

Processing flower 19, petal C

Finished rough-in on flower 19, petal C

Figures 8.97-8.98: This petal will not be as cupped or as detailed as the petals that are more visible. Do your best to keep it clean. Use the $^{25/3}$ backbend tool and the 3A/3 3mm spoon gouge to finish your rough-in. You can also get in with a 2mm straight gouge.

Figures 8.97-8.98: Process flower 19, petal A

Figures 8.99-8.102: Draw the ruffle lines and leaf veins. Petal D gets only one ruffle line. We will address petal A later.

Figure 8.99

Figure 8.100

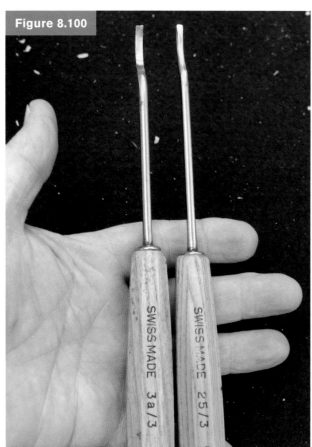

Figure 8.101

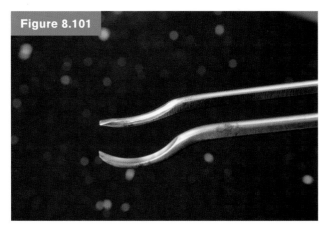

Figures 8.99-8.101: Tool for flower 19, petal A

Figure 8.102

Finished rough-in on petal A

Figure 8.103

Ruffle lines

Figures 8.103-8.104: Use the veiner tool to carve out the veins. Roll them over as in previous instructions. Petal A needs one groove in the center of the two over-petals. Create a shallow groove with a small diamond blade, then soften the edges. Detail the stamen as before.

Figure 8.104

Diamond bit

Figure 8.105

Finished Bloom #19

Chapter 9

MORE ABOUT UNDERCUTTING

Figure 9.1

22mm gouge

Figure 9.2

Backbend gouge

Figures 9.1-9.2: Undercutting is one of the most satisfying parts of this project because we see our work come to life. The undercutting work needs to be designed, making sure there is an even flow when viewed from different directions.

Let's begin with the left side of **flowers 17** and **18**. Petals A and D on both blooms are at the top of this cluster. Work toward the bottom to ensure that your most delicate work won't be disturbed. Begin roughing out with a 16–22mm 3-sweep gouge and mallet.

We will also use a 12mm backbend gouge. Scrape away all the material you can with these rough-in tools. Don't worry about shape yet.

Figure 9.3

Figure 9.4

Figures 9.3-9.5: Roughing in flowers 17 and 18

Figure 9.5

Figure 9.3-9.5: Imagine where your stem should attach itself under the bloom and stay away from this area. You want to create the illusion that the stem supports this area, even if a pod actually supports it. In other words, you don't want to look underneath and see nothing where a stem should be.

Figure 9.6: Keep the background clean with a 5A/8 spoon gouge. Remember to keep the contour with the background shape (don't carve this flat). We will smooth all undercutting areas out later. For now, let's do the gouge work all around the cluster.

Draw in the stem that goes under flowers 18 and 20, and begin roughing it in with a small kutzit burr.

Finished rough-in on left side

Figures 9.7-9.10: Start working toward your stem lines with a $^{25}\!/_{3}$ backbend and a small gouge. Then round over the stem of flower 18. You won't have to carve the stem very far under because this bloom is tilting down toward the stem, making it hard to see underneath.

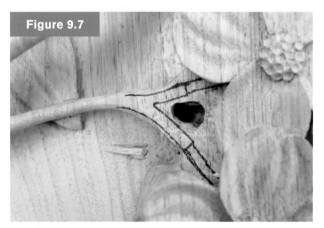

Drawing the stem

Stem detailing

Small kutzit burr bit

Roughing in the stem

Figure 9.11

Roughing in the stem with smaller bit

Figures 9.11-9.13: Using a small carbide bit, clean out between the stem's fork stem. This bit creates a nice shape. You can also use a ⅛" burr bit to help with the job.

Figure 9.12

Fork clean-out

Figure 9.13

Stem detailing

Figures 9.14-9.15: After you have rounded your stem, cut 220-grit sandpaper in ¼-wide strips. Thread a strip under the stem and gently sand back and forth underneath the stem.

We will continue to go around this cluster with our straight gouge. When the underwork is in tight areas, 6–8mm gouges work well. Use your backbend gouges, too.

Figure 9.14

Sand under stem

Figure 9.15

Finished stem

Figure 9.16-9.17: I am using a 6mm straight gouge and a small backbend gouge for this portion of undercutting work.

Figure 9.16

Figure 9.17

Figures 9.16-9.17: Roughing in flower 20

Figures 9.18-9.19: Moving on to **flower 20**, use power to rough-in petal D's bottom right side. Power out with a larger burr on the top petal C, since the grains cross the angle of your tools. Carving with power puts less pressure on the wood than gouges do. However, be sure you have good control of your power tool, or you may damage the piece.

Figure 9.18

Figure 9.19

Powering out right side of flower 20

Finished rough-in on right side of flower 20

Figure 9.20

Figure 9.20: Use a large burr to power out between flowers 20 and 18. Clean up under both flowers after powering through.

Powering out flower 20, petal C

Figure 9.21

Figure 9.22

Figure 9.23

Figure 9.24

Figure 9.21-9.24: Flowers 19 and 17 are low to the background and will not be very visible, so their right sides will be wedged out in a bevel shape. (The ability to judge what is important and what isn't is a vital part of wood carving, or any medium.)

Powering between flower 20 and 18

Wedging out flowers 17 and 19

Finish Wedge-out undercutting

Figures 9.25-9.26: Use the backbend gouge on the top of this cluster and a small, straight gouge for clean-out. The straight gouge can also be a scraper tool the same as we used it around the bottom leaf clusters.

Undercutting at top of cluster

Power-finish undercutting

Figure 9.27: The final undercutting step is done with power carving. I use three diamond bit sizes: $1/16$", $1/8$", and $1/4$". Since the basic shape is already finished, simply go back over all of the powered areas and clean them once more for a smoother look. No sanding is required in your undercut areas.

To clean up your background around your flower supports, use a 5-sweep gouge.

Figures 9.28-9.29: The following photos show how to undercut all the areas. Once you have completed the cluster that I have just taken you through, you won't have any problems with the rest. It will be a lot of the same process. Most of the outside of the cluster work will be wedged out, while most of the inside work will be powered out.

Figures 9.28-9.29: Gouge work on floor-to-flower support

Figures 9.30-9.53: First, we will take a look at **flowers 1 and 2**. The rest of the undercutting on this project uses the same process. The following images show completion of the entire sculpture.

Undercutting flowers 1 and 2

Undercutting flowers 3 and 6

Inside cluster

Flower 4

Flower 5

Flowers 7 and 8

Flower 6

Flower 7

Figure 9.40

Flowers 9–16

Figure 9.41

Flowers 9–12, inside cluster

Figure 9.42

Fowers 13–16 from top of cluster

Figure 9.43

Flowers 17 and 18 outside cluster

Figure 9.44

Flowers 17, 18, and 20

Figure 9.45

Finished flowers 1 and 2

Figure 9.46

Flowers 17–20, outside Cluster

Figure 9.47

Finished flowers 7 and 8

Figure 9.48

Finished flowers 3 and 6

Figure 9.49

Finished flower 5

Figure 9.52

Finished flowers 17–20

Figure 9.50

Finished flowers 9, 10, 11, 12, and 15

Figure 9.51

Finished flowers 13, 14, and 16

Figure 9.53

Finished carving

Chapter 10

ADDING COLOR

Bleaching

Figure 10.1-10.4: Use Klean Strip® two-part wood bleach to bleach out the petals. Mix equal parts A and B. Put very little on your brush. It is water-thin and should not touch anything but the petals. Dampen the petals and let them dry overnight; then determine if you want to bleach them again to create a lighter color (I bleached my dogwoods twice). Let them dry again and sand lightly with 220-grit sandpaper.

Figure 10.1

Wood bleach

Figure 10.2

Bleaching

Figure 10.3

Bleached petal

Figure 10.4

Finished bleaching

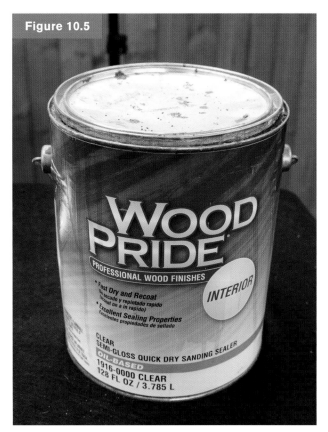

Figure 10.5

Sealer

Figure 10.6

Sealing the carving

Sealing

Figures 10.5-10.7: I like to use oil-based products, but it is getting harder to find them. I use Wood Pride® for all of my carving projects. Using various size brushes, apply the sealer to the entire woodcarving. Let the carving dry overnight and lightly sand with 220-grit sandpaper.

Figure 10.7

Sanded sealer

Painting the Petals

Figure 10.8: The paint colors in the remaining steps are from Hobby Lobby, but all brands of craft paints offer the color names specified. Use Titanium White for the petals. Thin the paint with Liquin® and paint the petals. Next, dip a brush in the thinner and brush back over the petals, taking most of the white off. Rather than covering up the beautiful butternut wood grains, you want to enhance them with color.

Figure 10.8

Painting the petals

Figures 10.09-10.13: Paint the stamen with Sap Green and let dry. Use a 1:1 mixture of Sap Green and White to paint the hollows as demonstrated in figure 10-10. Next, use very small dots of white, yellow, and brown to finish off the stamen. Using Van Dyke Brown, rake upward lightly at the tip notch to create a burnt tip look.

Figure 10.9

Paint the stamen

Figure 10.10

Painting the hollows

Figure 10.11

Stamen dots

Figure 10.12

Finished dots

Figure 10.13

Painting the tip

Painting the Stamen

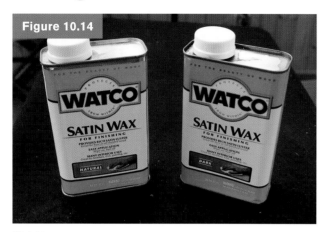

Figure 10.14

Finishing wax

Figure 10.15

Highlighting the stem

Leaf and Stem

Figures 10.14-10.15: Mix Sap Green with thinner and apply to the entire stem and leaves, then wipe them off and let them dry. Use Warm Gray paint to highlight the stem and brush in. Hightlight the stem joints with touches of brown.

When dry, finish the carving with Watco Satin Wax. I used dark wax on the background and natural wax on the entire stem.

Using various size brushes, apply a thin coat of wax; wait a few minutes and wipe off with a small cloth. Caution: Use a small cloth that won't catch on the carvings.

Figure 10.16

• SPRING BLOSSOMS •

Chapter 11

BUILDING THE FRAME

Inner Frame

Figure 11.1

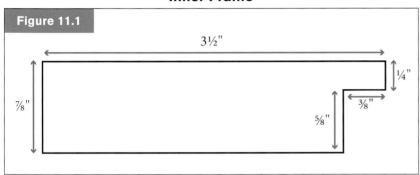

Inner frame

Figure 11.2

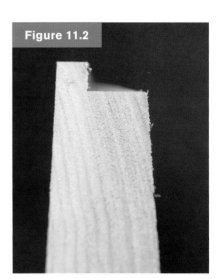

Rabbit

Figure 11.1-11.2: I chose black walnut wood for the frame because it complements the butternut. You'll need four pieces of 3½" stock cut 24" long. Sand the front and back down to 80 grit with an orbital sander. We will rabbit out the edges.

Rip ¼" horizontally (toward the carving) by ½" vertically if your stock is ¾" thick. Next, cut the end on a 45-degree miter.

Figure 11.3

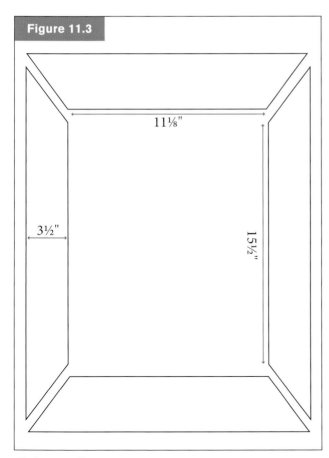

45-degree miters

Figure 11.4

Clamp miters

Figure 11.3-11.4: Start a little long and dry-fit your pieces. They should have ⅛" play so your carving has room to expand. When everything fits, glue the joints and place them in clamping miters overnight.

Remove the clamps using even pressure so you do not put too much pressure on any one part. The frame is unstable at this point, so be careful handling it. Pre-bore a ⅛" hole through the edge and into both joints. Countersink and install 3" screws.

Figures 11.5-11.6: Lay four 3½×3½" L brackets on the corners and outline their footprint. Rout out so the bracket lies flush with the wood. Make sure the screws are short enough so they won't go through the front of the frame.

Figure 11.5

Figures: 11.5-11.6: Install screws

Figure 11.6

Figure 11.7: Now we are ready to build the outer frame. Rip four pieces 2¾" wide and 24" long. Rabbit out as shown in figure 11.8.

Figure 11.7

Brackets installed

Outer Frame

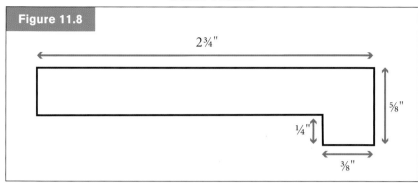

Figure 11.8

2¾"

⅝"

¼"

⅜"

Outer frame

Figures 11.8-11.12: Clamp the four pieces over the inner frame using the same bar clamps. This time, add glue to the edge and install thin wedges. Let this set overnight and add blocks to each corner. Glue and screw into both pieces of the outer frame (figure 11.12).

Figure 11.9

Rabbited-out outer frame

Figure 11.10

Outer frame

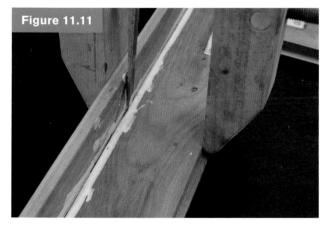

Figure 11.11

Wedge and glue

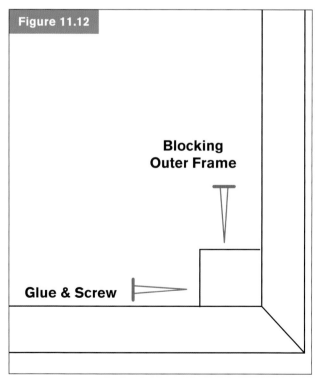

Figure 11.12

Blocking Outer Frame

Glue & Screw

Blocking the outer frame

Figures 11.13-11.15: Sand the entire frame to 600 grit, pre-finish with walnut stain, seal, and finish. I use a hand-rubbed lacquer finish, but you can use anything clear. Use a small L bracket to install the carving. The bracket does not fasten tightly against the carving, allowing the wood to expand.

Figure 11.13

Figure 11.14

Finished frame

Figure 11.15

Fasten carving

Chapter 12

BEGINNER DOGWOOD STEM

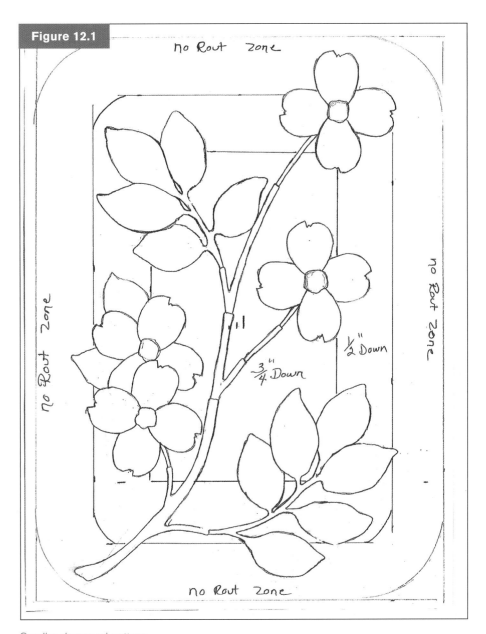

Smaller dogwood pattern

Figure 12.1: This smaller carving pattern can serve as a test run. My students complete it in three 8-hour days. I recommend taking plenty of time to become familiar with the techniques before going on to the larger carving in this book.

This carving is done with 1" thick carving stock. Figure 12-1 shows you the routing pattern. Simply follow the chapter-by-chapter instructions of the main project. Use the picture as a guide, but give the stem its own personality and shape and turn the flowers any way you wish.

The picture in this book was done in basswood. Routed blanks for the small and large carving are available at Walker Wood Carving, which you can call at 479-474-0813 or 479-459-0813. Finished pieces are also offered, as are classes for 10–20 people.

Cut in the Background

Watch your grain pattern.
• Use a #4 (25mm) gouge and let your router lines be your guide.
• Use a #2 sweep (8mm) gouge and your knife for stop cuts.

Stylize flowers, stems, and leaves

• Use #3 and #5 sweeps. The higher you keep your carving, the more time you will spend undercutting.

Watch your grain pattern.
• Redraw your pattern using a paper template.
• Clean up the flower circumference.
• Use a knife and small #2, #2, and #5 gouges. Be sure to shave this and don't gouge out.

Don't gouge out all the way to the background—shave out a little at a time.
• Separate and shape leaves.
• More stylizing for this operation. Use small gouges and knife. Draw in the veins and leaves, groove out the veins, and then soften using a small flat palm gouge.

Shape the Flower

Relieve out the petals, going deep enough to raise the stamen. Draw in the veins; groove out and smooth with a small flat gouge.

Shape the stem

Be careful here. Work with the grain using very sharp tools. Be sure to shave rather than gouge.

Undercut

• Power out all you can, and then clean up using your knife, 7 L/6 bent gouge, and backward gouges.
• *Key: Shave out a little at a time.*
• Sand with 220 wet/dry paper, folded to make a sharp edge.
• *Key: Consider the paper another tool; you can easily damage your carving with it.*

Finalize the Background

• Work with the grain as best as you can.
• *The hand sees better than the eye.*

Paint

Flowers:
• 1 Part Titanium White
• ¼ part Unbleached Titanium

Leaves:
• 1 part Oxide of Chromium
• ½ part Prussian Green
• ¼ part Unbleached Titanium

Stems:
• 1 part Brown Madder (Alizarin)
• 1 part Burnt Sienna
• 1 part Van Dyke Brown
• Use Liquin to thin the oil paint and accelerate drying.

Finish the Beginner Carving

Seal your carving with:
• Wood Pride interior oil-based semi-gloss quick-dry sanding sealer (800-984-5444)
• Watco Satin Wax (800-635-3286)
• Watco Danish Oil (800-635-3286)
• Klean Strip Wood Bleach (800-238-2672)

Steps:
1. Apply bleach to the flower petals (do this step only when carving with butternut).
2. Apply natural Danish oil to the background.
3. Seal the flowers, leaves, and stem.
4. Add color to the flowers, leaves, and stems.
5. Wax the entire carving.

Chapter 13:

GALLERY

Boundless Passion. Inspired by the poem "The Legend of the Dogwood," this carving taught me just how far I could go with deep relief. When carving the center leaf cluster, I kept going farther and farther in, using gouges only, until I hollowed out the entire leaf cluster.

Mesa Verde. The Mesa Verde ruins inspired me to create this relief in a piece of maple I brought home from Oregon.

Bald Eagle. This sculpture is 4" thick from the beak to the back.

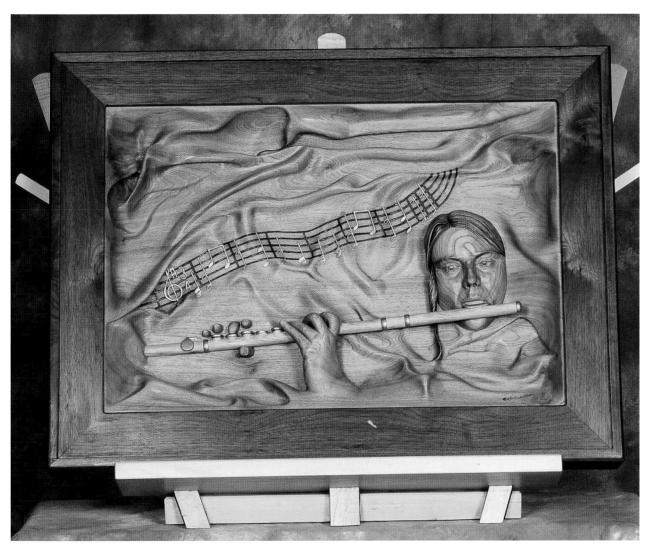

Amazing Grace. My daughter, a flutist, posed for this carving. In the background are musical notes from the first line of *Amazing Grace.*

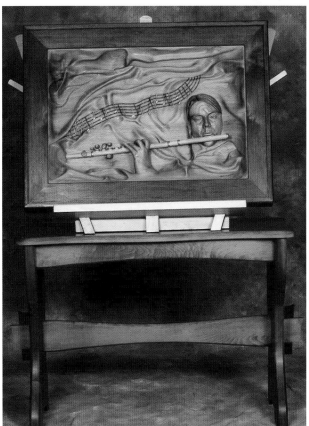

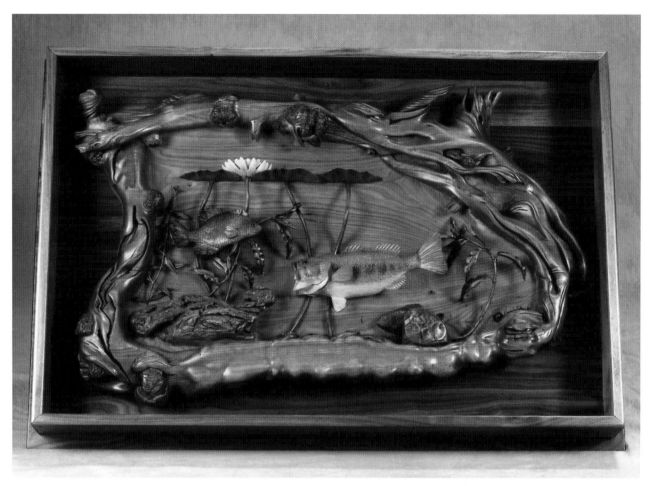

No Compromise. This is a deep relief with no attachments and was inspired by an underwater picture of a bass in a standoff with a crawdad. It is 5" deep, roughly 30" high, and 4' wide.

SPRING BLOSSOMS

Spring Blossoms

Delicato Fiore. This butternut carving was done in deep relief except for two blooms and the abstract fire-like foliage coming up from behind the stems. I inlayed turquoise and metal in the corners. The frame is cherry.

Author bio

Kevin Walker started carving in 1982. He was influenced mostly by the relief carving he saw in Branson, Missouri, and went on to develop his technique in extreme high-relief woodcarving. more or less exclusive in this area of sculpture, has sold his work to galleries such as the Natior Museum of Woodcarvers in Custer, South Dako Pete Engler Designs in Branson, Missouri; and several private collectors nationwide. Each piec one-of-a-kind, and the drafting, wood preparat and finishes are his own handwork. The carving are single slab—deep relief carvings with no pie glued or attached. He does not reproduce any o work. To see more of the author's work, visit www.walkerwoodcarving.com